FOREWORD

Riff grew out of a brief flash of an idea about a poem that never ended but instead meandered to and fro, buffeted, and gave us what you'll discover on each page of this issue.

With that seed of inspiration in mind, we decided to see what would happen if we gave poets the same starting and finishing line. What would grow to fill that strange space between beginning and end?

Magic, as it turns out.

While each poem included in this issue speaks with its own unique voice, just like a choir, they come together in harmony at the chorus. I don't know about you, but my sappy soul finds great comfort and profound joy in that.

I want to thank every one of our featured poets for adding their words to our jam session. Sending a warm thanks to everyone who had a hand in making this issue a reality, especially NaBeela Washington for letting me help out in producing this issue and for being a vibrant, caring, and visionary light.

And thank you for reading. I hope you turn on a favorite song, sit back, and enjoy.

BRANDON MCWILLIAMS
GUEST EDITOR

Copyright © 2021 *Lucky Jefferson*.

All rights reserved. This book or any portion thereof may not be reproduced or used in any manner whatsoever without the express written permission of the publisher except for the use of brief quotations in a book review.

Printed in the United States of America.

ISBN 978-0-578-88734-0

ISSUE DESIGN and PROOFREADING by NaBeela Washington
GUEST EDITING by Brandon McWilliams
COVER ART by Shang-Te Chen and Ikirya Lane
ALTERNATE COVER ART (p2) by Rice Gallardo

Shang-Te Chen [Ted] is a designer from Taiwan who majors in Interaction Design at California College of the Arts. He draws illustrations, watches horror movies, and floats in his daydreams. Follow Ted by visiting shangtechen.com.

Ikirya Lane is a recent graduate from Towson University and received a degree in Digital Art and Design with a focus in Animation.

Rice Gallardo is a junior at The School of Visual Arts New York City and is pursuing a BFA in Illustration.

Publication of *Lucky Jefferson* is made possible through community support.

Donate or submit to *Lucky Jefferson* on our website: luckyjefferson.com.

SET LIST

ANTHEMS OF ANCESTORS	JEAN FINEBERG
WHAT NINA DOES TO ME	DEVONAE J. MANDERSON
TRADING FOURS WE BE	CATHERINE LEE
HOURI	CHARLENE STEGMAN MOSKAL
JEREMIAH THE BULLFROG	RESI IBAÑEZ
INVOCATIONS IN EB7#9	RAPHAEL JENKINS
IMPROVISATION	STEVE GERSON
SOMETIMES I SHAKE TOO	KATIE MANNING
DAY THUMPS DOWN	JOHN DAVIS
A BACKYARD BRAZILIAN BIRTHDAY PARTY	LISSA BATISTA
STOLEN TIME	ROBERT WALTERS
EXIT MUSIC	MATT SCHROEDER
HAIRBRUSH BOOT GRIND	KATIE KEMPLE
ASSASSIN	JANET JIAHUI WU
NIGHTS AT THE COURT	DAVID HIGDON

A burst of sudden tempo evokes tremors.
Cowbell pumps the clave, congas dive in,
muscles engage, and couples flood the floor.

Heartbeats sync with Latin rhythms, recalling
la patria, where the anthems of ancestors
seep through stones and walls.

Bongos spark memories of homemade
tamboras, fashioned from buckets and
coaxed into life by field-browned hands.

Trumpets proclaim proud fanfares
as three generations of facile fingers
fire the valves in familial tandem.

The guitarrón, with its sonorous bass power,
becomes the chassis, and drives the thrumming
train, while children strum small guitars.

Hand-bored wooden flutes, abuelos to all
the instruments, flutter like folksy filigree,
and are said to communicate with birds.

The seamless stream of salsa, rumba and
meringue lasts until dawn, when a
beguiling bolero signals time to rest.

Lovers lay weary heads on shoulders,
as bodies entwine and sway to
rubato rhythms, inclined ears exalt.

ANTHEMS OF ANCESTORS **JEAN FINEBERG**

A burst of sudden tempo evokes tremors
rising from throat onto tongue
shaking our black bodies
effortlessly
like earthquake
like trees uprooted in
a belly deep vibrato
in belly deep shrills
and whoops
there are men snapping
and women clapping
everybody's feet stomping
you wonder why your mother tried so hard to keep you away
from this
this magic thing
this thing that courses through you
moving your hips
rolling your eyes back
gripping your neck
catching your breath at the back of your throat
before it can reach your tongue
before you begin to hum
listen to the magic man sing
with his trumpet in
rubato rhythms, inclined ears exalt

COMPOSER

WHAT NINA DOES TO ME   **DEVONAE J. MANDERSON**

A burst of sudden tempo evokes tremors,
lines weaving trumpets, alto saxes,
trombone, vibraphone, percussion
genius jams. These cats instruct us,
taking turns trading fours,
with obbligato excellence.
We be hearing disengagement
from toxic marshals
justifying doing lethal harm
just following unequal martial laws.
We be yielding
not to tired tempered scale
of patriarchal papas snuffing breaths.
Nope, dope
peace, with dark-skinned peoples
we be one in music loveship,
When jazz tells tales of
humans being relations, some
body better be hearing hard,
rubato rhythms, inclined ears exalt

TRADING FOURS WE BE   **CATHERINE LEE**

A burst of sudden tempo evokes tremors -
I feel his hands touch me in my places,
ebony dark as secrets,
ivory pale as blank pages.
I become something larger than sound
alive with anticipation,
aware that he plays me like a lover,
familiar and precious.
I soar under the vibrato his hands awaken -
brings me to thunder low and rich,
takes me high to warble like bird song.
I am what he needs me to be,
his messenger without words.
I am what I have been made for,
an houri to heighten love,
bring beauty to those who listen.
And in the end, before it is over
he quiets me lightly, softly,
a whisper of spent passion,
rubato rhythms, inclined ears exalt.

COMPOSER

HOURI CHARLENE STEGMAN MOSKAL

A burst of sudden tempo evokes tremors
Brass blaring, I blink bleary eyes
and wake up to stadium suns,
cold night astroturf beneath my feet.
A dropped baton cracked my skull, and opened, my throat
lets out an off key rumble from
the lowest regions of my basso profundo. Deepest diaphragm belly bellows
cracked drumskin makes me a croaking amphibian.
I gasp for air breathing my alternate tuning,
my glissandos less graceful, more hopping
from one lilypad note to another.
I am a percussion frog drumhead ache -
catching rain in my mouth.
Work your pressure, your mallets, on me, your new tympanic lake,
hear my moans ground the brass and woodwind forest that surrounds you.
Broken I am a new sound --
learn how I sing,
play with me and I will leapfrog with you:
up and down, back and forth, listen for my
rubato rhythms, inclined ears exalt

JEREMIAH THE BULLFROG   RESI IBAÑEZ

INTERMISSION

LUCKY JEFFERSON'S LITERARY ARTISTS:

Katie Le + Denni Long designed the artwork on the next page.

Katie Le enjoys creating stories through whimsical and painterly Illustrations that she hopes to share with others to bring forth smiles.

Follow Katie at
katiekle.wixsite.com/portfolio.

Denni Long pursues a BFA in Communications Design, with an emphasis in Illustration, at Pratt Institute.

NOTE YOUR REACTION:

What was your favorite piece in this set?

A burst of sudden tempo evokes tremors
from dusty floorboards clean up
to the tin roof that becomes our
ancestors' dance floor at twilight.
Charlestons & mashed potatoes
rain; their patters, the percussive push
setting pace for moaning horns to
pontificate in this ramshackle
palace—high-hats for support
beams, minor chords
waxing the floors to mirrors.
From the brass mouth of a sax
leaps a humid breath whose tenor
arches its back in beckoning. A
bedazzled songbird heeds the call;
flying in, landing on the downbeat,
spotlight catching the gems in her
feathers. Born with a shotgun for
a throat, she aims her ode toward
a skylight installed after her debut,
& pumps a melisma of buckshots
into the dance-move-downpour
swaddling this sanctuary. Her holler
folds into the delicious
cacophony of sweat & whiskey-addled
rubato rhythms, inclined ears exalt

COMPOSER

INVOCATIONS IN E♭7#9 **RAPHAEL JENKINS**

A burst of sudden tempo evokes tremors
that pulse like bass beat thrums

fingers and thumb as hands along your back
each bone a note my body sings and zing

the bend of riff your sway into my arms' embrace
I feel your breath and sigh the melody stretching

giving going our love and sensuously your name in song
from my lips sips as saxophone wails and funk pop drop

then the drumming of tap and brush along your shoulders
the snap of snares like birds caught on wing we entangled

in with of our palms intertwined heat hard and skin soft
your voice the croon as from a beer-soaked microphone

my call and response we in syncopated dance
our harmonic discordance of jangling notes aligning misaligned

quaver along the staff of clef sharp breath mark trill and turn
slurring accented up bow down bow my fingers through your hair

like strumming fretboard strings your nails along my ribs
like piano keys plunging in this improvisation as love as life

I whisper your name you whisper my name anxiously
rubato rhythms, inclined ears exalt

IMPROVISATION　　　　　**STEVE GERSON**

A burst of sudden tempo evokes tremors,
and as the blast of brass vibrates
through the auditorium floor, up
the armrests, and into my hands,
I think of you, the band director
who stepped in to conduct my
college choir mid-year when we
were left without a leader; you,
whose hands never stopped
keeping their own time against
your will; you, who never let
the shaking stop us from taking
deep breaths, unfolding trembling
timbres to layer waves together
in the air; you, who could shift
the quality of sixty tones just
by opening one pulsing palm.
You're somehow still alive to me
in sound, surprise syncopation,
rubato rhythms, inclined ears exalt.

SOMETIMES I SHAKE TOO   **KATIE MANNING**
for Dan Nelson

A burst of sudden tempo evokes tremors
on the dancefloor. All a woman can do
is flail her arms like scraps of trash.
The night, chromed, becomes a lowrider

shifting gears, blasting caps out its exhaust pipe.
Onstage the harmonica man slaps
a burring rhythm into his solo, early dance
of death, red as ripe tomatoes, a one-man

wrecking crew disinfecting windfalls,
peeling swatches of birch bark, a grunt
and grind beyond the gin and tonics,
the tequila shooters, the branched-up

hairdos flaring beside the bar. If you
arrived for a quadrangle of love, this
is not your night not for autumn moonlight
not for lilied voices. Not a night

when you weigh how much water
makes up your body. This is the tectonic
shift of singe and sweat that clears
memory, the balance that counters

balance, breath tasting breath
inside a harmonica reed with speed
hunking down the disco ball:
rubato rhythms, inclined ears exalt.

COMPOSER

DAY THUMPS DOWN   **JOHN DAVIS**

A burst of sudden tempo evokes tremors
on the vibrating dirt floor, our feet, bare
with black bottoms, the balls pestling
into the earth as if we can grind ourselves
into each other and root with rhythm
our mothers taught us when we bounced
breast to shoulder; a body lullabye.
Our tia rounds her waist in circles,
her mouth open and singing, she's a tuba
with deep guttural sounds she bellows,
her arms are raised in conversation
with her body, playing the crowd a concert--
It's a house party on a weekday and all
the neighbors and neighboring come
for the 3-liter frosted *Skols* and *picanhas*
but they stay for the *Forro* or *Pagode*,
You'll need a *cavaco, o surdo, tan-tan*,
but most importantly. the *hand-repique*,
      the steel drum;
they call her the most beautiful one, the one
you need to use both hands on the skin
and the body of the drum-- she is heard over
everyone's voices, stirs the people to scrape
their feet, either to mimic or in jealousy.
It doesn't matter. We all samba; half-rainbowed
      rubato rhythms, inclined ears exalt.

A BACKYARD BRAZILIAN BIRTHDAY PARTY   LISSA BATISTA

INTERMISSION

LUCKY JEFFERSON'S LITERARY ARTISTS:

Jenna Kwon + Jordan Hillman designed the artwork on the next page.

Formally known as "Na Young", **Jenna Kwon** was born in Korea, but was raised most of her life in Kansas City.

She currently attends college at ArtCenter College of Design majoring in Illustration Design, but hopes to explore and expand her skills from other fields. She likes to read poems and hangout with her mom and her pet Peanut during her free time.

Follow Jenna at kwonniestudio.com.

Jordan Hillman [He/ They] is an art student at Herron School of Art and Design.

WRITING PROMPT:

Write a poem about your favorite concert memory.

A burst of sudden tempo evokes tremors,
beat within beat, stolen time inside the
rubato rhythms, inclined ears exalt!

We are at first frightened by this fierce
notion that we must move or be lost when
A burst of sudden tempo evokes tremors

within our core, so we dance seeking
spaces between spaces between beats,
rubato rhythms, inclined ears exalt

to hear the sound our wild hearts seek,
the urgent cadence we need to thrive!
A burst of sudden tempo evokes tremors

that tell us we are alive and now must
seek the hidden places found inside
rubato rhythms, inclined ears exalt,

listening to the fullness of the sounds
within the flow that feeds our being...
A burst of sudden tempo evokes tremors,

for we are nothing if not creatures of
pulsing, moving, dancing, driving
rubato rhythms, inclined ears exalt!

STOLEN TIME   **ROBERT WALTERS**

A burst of sudden tempo evokes tremors
        as a lonely bassoon begins its soft honk
                of triplets that seek to whelm   over

        wind chiming through a piano's strings
under   the fingernails of a musician holding
        a mallet & dragging the back end across

            said strings while hitting wool yarn
        against the rosewood of a marimba
that is   against the history of a forest

        whole notes interspersed & swirling
            through air by a brass resonator   dancing
        as if birdsong falling through the trees

a sharp melody cuts through the soft wilderness
        the tinny arrival of muted trumpets &
            elephant romp of cartoonish trombones

        slipping upright in the mud as they
glissando quickly to their desired pitch
        as the sunlight of melody cuts through

            cymbals begin to ride in the distance
        like heatwave distortions that trick vision
a chain that hangs on in its constant sizzle

        the blackening screen & white names
            unimportant   the story told
        that is now nothing more than music

cannot measure to each drum that picks up
        this song that starts a new beginning
rubato rhythms   inclined ears exalt

COMPOSER

EXIT MUSIC   **MATT SCHROEDER**

A burst of sudden tempo evokes tremors
rubato rhythms, inclined ears exalt.

Jumping off loft beds onto hard floors
We transform hairbrushes into rackets

Slamming air filled balloons hard
they go slooooooooooow down the tempo

Flipping brushes like pancakes, we hit big
boom fantastic, timpani drum goes elastic.

A burst of sudden tempo evokes tremors
rubato rhythms, inclined ears exalt.

Evening crickets purr for more,
we leave windows open, open doors.

We click our too loud boots down sidewalks,
echoing like deserted high school hallways

We are the stars of these empty streets,
these stucco walls, these construction stalls.

A burst of sudden tempo evokes tremors
rubato rhythms, inclined ears exalt.

The beans fall into the grinder, rain stick
sounds wake us, we grind faster, faster

Bombastic destruction turns to caffeinated
laughter, what does it matter if we're up?

Feet stomp downstairs, utensils triangle.
Percussive plates crash to metal sinks after.

A burst of sudden tempo evokes tremors
rubato rhythms, inclined ears exalt.

COMPOSER

HAIRBRUSH BOOT GRIND   **KATIE KEMPLE**

A burst of sudden tempo evokes tremors:
room, that rook, strutting up and down the room
big round bottoms Tuscany Ligurian, Florence
on the wheel, wasting no time, colts bolt, dog balks
the singular women walk, basement case, spares
change going from hand to hand, making no demand
aches, phases, the rolling pin, bashing a head
in, segments of a caterpillar, worm, signals in the wire
basking legs, talk easy into the telephone, screens
screaming subtitles, roads to the church, rhubarbs
second classes, out of tune, fashion lugged, aye
rye, ain't right, busting, canning, rusted tins
no fear, no loathing, no room, beaten down
casement over that champs-elysees cafe, getting late
souvenir bikini girls, smooth glide down down
down, her toes, misty, smoky, baked the sax-
ophone, lento, oh ever so gentle a halt
rubato rhythms, inclined ears exalt

COMPOSER

ASSASSIN   JANET JIAHUI WU

A burst of sudden tempo evokes tremors.
It awakens the worms, makes the wolves
howl, heads lurched backward. Broken
glass and weeds fill my vertigo, streetlights
dance along the edge of periphery, soft focus,
a swirling bokeh, an aberration, strobes
against the sides of my consciousness.
Boys play ball, hustle, talk like grown men,
throw coins as girls walk by, pretend no
one exists, no one wants to be made an object.
Laugh, speed your pace, double Dutch,
hopscotch and jacks. Move fast. Don't look
up. Keep walking. To the box, beneath those
rubato rhythms, inclined ears exalt.

NIGHTS AT THE COURT **DAVID HIGDON**

WRITING PROMPT:

What musicians do you look forward to seeing perform live in the future? Write a poem about the way your favorite genre of music makes you feel.

ENCORE

WRITING PROMPT:

Use a line from your favorite poem in this issue to start a new story or poem.

LISTEN TO WHAT YOUR FELLOW COMPOSERS JAM TO

"La Mujer Latina", Latin Fever
"Take the A Train", Duke Ellington
"Four Women", Nina Simone
"Locomotion", John Coltrane
"Bebop", Charlie Parker
"Nobody Knows You When You're Down and Out", Jimmie Cox then Bessie Smith
"Moment's Notice", John Coltrane
"Rhapsody in Blue", George Gershwin
"Piece of My Heart", Janis Joplin
Household Sounds
"Bitter Fruit", The Kills
"Gold Soundz", Pavement
"The Rite of Spring", Igor Stravinsky and Vasily Petrenko
"Todo, Todo, Todo", Daniela Romo
"Chips Ahoy", The Hold Steady
"The Girl", Ipanema
"Nuit sur les Champs-Elysees" (1)-(4), Miles Davis
"I've Got to Use My Imagination", Gladys Knight and the Pips
"N Side", Steve Lacy
"They Want EFX", Das EFX

VISIT BIT.LY/RIFFONSPOTIFY OR

INSPIRATION:
What song(s) will you be adding to your playlist? What new ideas does this set list inspire?

WHAT'S NEXT

Upcoming Calls For Submissions:

Issue 7: *Cookout*

Grab your sunglasses, sandals, and favorite dish—you're invited to our cookout.

For this collaborative potluck issue, send us your unpublished poetry (there is no line limit but we adore shorter poems), flash fiction, and food-inspired art that describes what you would bring to our cookout.

Topics may include:

- food
- games / entertainment
- libations
- decorations
- cutlery

The world is your oyster. So get creative, pull up a chair, and settle in.

All submissions will be used to create a reflective spread of literary treats for our party.

Early Bird Submissions (free): April 1 - May 31
Last Call Submissions ($2): June 1-15
Accepted Writers Announced: Mid-July 2021

FOLLOW US ONLINE

 @lucky_jefferson

 @luckyjeffersonlit

 @_luckyjefferson

USE #RIFF
& #LJSQUAD
TO FOLLOW THE
CONVERSATION

+

TAKE A SELFIE
WITH YOUR COPY
OF RIFF AND TAG US!

www.ingramcontent.com/pod-product-compliance
Lightning Source LLC
Chambersburg PA
CBHW071417290426
44108CB00014B/1864